1 MONTH OF
FREE
READING

at
www.ForgottenBooks.com

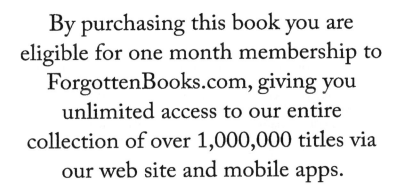

By purchasing this book you are eligible for one month membership to ForgottenBooks.com, giving you unlimited access to our entire collection of over 1,000,000 titles via our web site and mobile apps.

To claim your free month visit:

www.forgottenbooks.com/free889693

ISBN 978-0-265-78992-6
PIBN 10889693

Historic, archived document

Do not assume content reflects current
scientific knowledge, policies, or practices.

D. M. FERRY & CO'S

WHOLESALE LIST

OF

FOR

1892

D. M. FERRY & CO.

SEEDSMEN,

DETROIT, - - - MICHIGAN.

TO THE TRADE.

In presenting our **Annual Wholesale Price List of Seeds in Bulk for 1892,** we beg to call your attention to the following points as being worthy of your most serious consideration, in connection with placing your order for the year's supply of bulk seeds. We are, by far, the largest growers of Vegetable Seeds in this country, having much land of our own devoted to this purpose, and thousands of acres grown each year under contract, by skilful growers. We have also a large farm where stock seeds are grown, (these are the seeds we furnish our growers to plant for us.) We are very careful to have the different kinds of seeds grown in such localities, and on such soils as are adapted to their most perfect development. The growing crops are all visited during the season, and samples of all the stocks used are planted on our Trial Grounds as an additional check. By these means we are enabled to know, as nearly as it is possible, the exact quality of the seeds we offer. In short, we do everything labor and expense can accomplish, toward making our seeds of such high quality that none better can be found.

Our prices are as low as Seeds of equal quality can be afforded. We again refer dealers to our motto, viz.: **THE BEST IS ALWAYS THE CHEAPEST.**

We send out only goods that will, to the best of our belief, give entire satisfaction; absolute immunity from error, however, being unattainable and success always being largely dependent on outside influences, it must be expressly understood that we give no warranty, express or implied, as to description, quality, productiveness, or any other matter connected with the goods we send out, and we will not be in anyway responsible for the crop.

If the purchaser does not accept the goods on these terms they must be returned at once.

Proportionately higher prices will be charged for quantities less than ¼ lb. or ¼ bu.

Where two qualities of any variety are quoted, the best will always be sent, unless specially otherwise ordered.

☞Not bound by these prices for any definite time or quantity and subject to advance without notice.

TERMS—Net Cash June 1, 1892, without regard to date of purchase, or a discount of one per cent. per month on the unexpired time when paid before maturity.

Bills amounting to less than $50 are net cash.

Field Peas, Clover, Hungarian, Millet, Timothy and all Grass Seeds, net cash, without any discount whatever.

CASH or satisfactory references must accompany orders from unknown correspondents.

DETROIT, January 12th, 1892. **D. M. FERRY & CO.**

☞**For Telegraphic Cipher Code, see inside last Cover Page.**

O. S. GULLEY, BORNMAN & CO.,
PRINTERS, DETROIT.

WHOLESALE PRICE LIST

.. OF ..

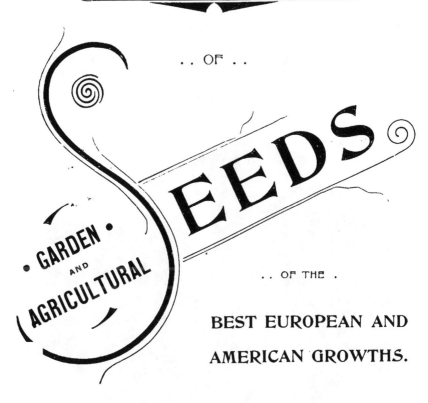

SEEDS

GARDEN AND AGRICULTURAL

.. OF THE .

BEST EUROPEAN AND AMERICAN GROWTHS.

OFFERED BY

D. M. FERRY & CO.,

SEEDSMEN,

DETROIT, - - MICHIGAN.

D. M. FERRY & CO'S
WHOLESALE PRICE LIST.

Challenge Dwarf Black Wax, Extra Early.

We wish to reiterate and emphasize our claims of last year for this grand new Bean. for another season's most thorough trial has more than justified everything we have said in praise of it. Its great vigor and prolificness, together with its extreme earliness and the uniformity with which the pods ripen, make it the best Wax Bean for the early crop. We are headquarters for this Bean, as almost the entire stock in the country is in our hands. **Per Bushel, $5.50.**

☞All varieties in **heavy face type** are of superior quality.

	Tel. Cipher.	Per Lb.
ARTICHOKE—		
Large Globe....................................	Accomack..	$3 00
ASPARAGUS—		
Conover's Colossal.............................	Addison.....	20
Roots, two years old, per 1,000, $5.00....	Alachua..........	

BEANS, Dwarf—		Per Bu.
Challenge Dwarf Black Wax, Extra Early.......	Aiken.......	$5 50
Black Eyed Wax, *very early, beautiful white pods*........	Anoka	5 00
D. M. Ferry & Co's Detroit Wax, *rust proof*.....	Allamakee ..	4 50
Wardwell's Kidney Wax, *early and productive*....	Albany...	5 50
D. M. Ferry & Co's Golden Wax...............	Alamance ..	4 00
Prolific German Wax, Black Seeded	Albermarle .	4 50
Golden=Eyed Wax, *new, good shipper*.............	Aransas.....	5 00
German Wax, White Seeded........................	Anne........	4 50
Speckled Wax, *very hardy, extra fine for shell beans.*		
See next page····························	Angelina	4 50
Scarlet Flageolet Wax............................	Alpine.... ..	3 50
Violet Flagolet Wax, or Perfection Wax.............	Alturas.	3 50
Crystal White Wax....	Alameda.....	4 50
Extra Early Refugee, *the earliest green podded bean*...	Allegany....	3 50
Early Red Valentine, Improved Round Pod. See		
4th Page of Cover..............................	Alpena......	3 00
Early Yellow Six Weeks, Improved Round Pod.		
New, distinct; dry bean nearly round; pods shorter than Early Yellow Kidney Six Weeks; thick, fleshy, stringless, and are splendid shippers,...............................	Asotin.......	4 00
Early China Red Eye............................	Alexander...	2 50
Dwarf Horticultural, *very early*................	Andrew......	4 00
Goddard, or Boston Favorite, *very prolific*.......	Antelope	4 00
Early Yellow Kidney, Six Weeks	Anson	3 00
Early Mohawk................................	Allegan......	3 00
Refugee, or Thousand to One....:................	Apache......	3 00
Royal Dwarf Kidney	Aroostook. .	2 75
Large White Marrow, or Mountain................	Appling.....	3 00
Early Marrow Pea, or Dwarf White Navy.............	Ashley.......	2 50

BEANS, Pole or Running—		
White Crease Back, *very early and productive*........	Augusta.....	5 00
Rhode Island Crease Back, *splendid for green shelled beans*	Austin.......	4 00
London Horticultural.............................	Aurora.......	4 50
Brocton Pole, *hardy and prolific.*	Audubon.....	4 50
Early Golden Cluster Wax, *extra early*...........	Audrain.....	6 00
Dutch Case Knife.........	Attala........	5 00
Indian Chief, or Tall Black Wax.................	Banks.......	4 50

SPECKLED WAX.

The best Bean to follow Golden Wax or Prolific Black Wax. It you want to plant one variety to use for snaps, green shelled, and in the dry state, plant this, because it is the best general crop bean. Its long, cylindrical, waxy yellow, fleshy, stringless, delicately flavored pods are fit for use directly after the above named sorts and continue in bearing the longest of any. When the pods get too mature for snaps, they become beautifully splashed and streaked with crimson, making them remarkably handsome, and at this stage the beans are fit to eat shelled. The Dwarf Horticultural has always been the standard of excellence as a green shelled bean, but we can assure our customers that the Speckled Wax is fully equal to or even better than Dwarf Horticultural in this particular, while in hardiness of vine and quantity of yield, it is better beyond all comparison.

After years of trial and careful watching, we assert the above points ot superiority for this variety and we know that a single careful planting will convince anyone that its merits are not in the least overstated. **Per Bushel, $4.50.**

BEANS, Pole or Running—Continued.

	Tel. Cipher.	Per Bu.
Red Speckled Cut Short, or Corn Hill ......,.....	Barton......	$6 00
Kentucky Wonder *or Old Homestead*	Bandera...	Sold out.
White Runner...........	Bates.......	5 00
Scarlet Runner..	Barry....	Crop Failed.
Early Jersey Lima, *very early and desirable*...... .	Barnes......	6 00
Small White Lima, Carolina or Sieva.................	Bailey.	5 50
Dreer's Improved Lima.	Ballard.... .	6 00
Challenger Lima, *very productive, extra*......	Baraga. . .	6 50
Large White Lima......	Baker.......	5 00
King of the Garden Lima....	Baca........	6 50

BEET—

		Per Lb.
Early Egyptian Blood Turnip, *finest stock*.........	Bath.........	25
Early Eclipse, *choicest stock*....	Bay..	25

DETROIT DARK RED TURNIP.

D. M. FERRY & CO'S
HALF LONG BLOOD.

BEET—Continued.

	Tel. Cipher.	Per Lb.
Early Blood Turnip, *improved*	Beaver	25
Detroit Dark Red Turnip, *new and the best blood Turnip Beet*	Bryan	40
Dewing's Early Blood Turnip	Bedford	20
Bastian's Early Blood Turnip	Baxter	20
Edmand's Early Blood Turnip	Becker	25
Early Turnip Bassano, *true*	Baylor	20
D. M. Ferry & Co's Half Long Blood, *altogether the finest variety for fall and winter use*	Beaufort	50
Long Dark Blood, *improved*	Benton	20
Swiss Chard, or Sea Kale Beet	Bond	25
French White Sugar, Red Top, *best for cattle*	Berrien	15
French Yellow Sugar	Benzie	25
Lane's Imperial Sugar	Bertie	15
Vilmorin's Improved Imperial Sugar	Bexar	25
Long Red Mangel Wurzel	Bibb	18
D. M. Ferry & Co's Improved Mammoth Long Red Mangel Wurzel, Per 100 lbs., $15.00	Bladen	20
Norbitan Giant Long Red Mangel Wurzel	Blair	20
Yellow Globe Mangel Wurzel	Blanco	18
Carter's Warden Prize Yellow Globe Mangel Wurzel	Bland	18
Yellow Leviathan Mangel Wurzel	Blaine	25
Yellow Ovoid Mangel Wurzel	Bledsoe	15
Golden Tankard Mangel Wurzel	Blount	18
Red Globe Mangel Wurzel	Boise	15

BROCOLI—

Early Purple Cape	Boone	2 00

BRUSSELS SPROUTS—

Best Imported	Bowie	1 50

CABBAGE—

FIRST EARLY SORTS.

Extra Early Express, *the earliest Cabbage yet produced*	Boyle	1 50
Early Jersey Wakefield, *best American seed*	Broome	1 50
Early Jersey Wakefield, *true, good stock*	Brown	1 00
Very Early Etampes	Brooks	1 25
Early York	Brazos	1 25
Early Large York	Bremer	1 25
Henderson's Early Summer, *true, finest stock*	Brule	1 25
Early Dwarf Flat Dutch, *extra fine for summer use; try it*	Bucks	1 50
Early Winnigstadt, *true*	Burke	1 25
German Filderkraut	Burnet	1 75
All Seasons, *very desirable, reliable in heading*	Buchanan	1 50
Succession, *extra stock*	Brevard	2 25

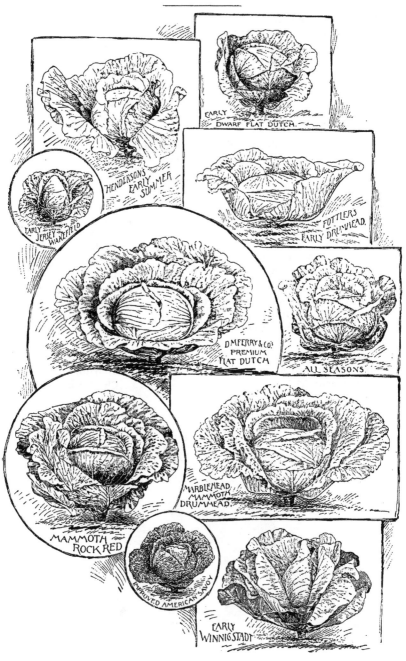

CABBAGE—Continued.   Tel. Cipher.   Per

Fottler's Early Drumhead or Brunswick Short
     Stem, *true American, splendid stock* ....**Caddo** $1

Fottler's Early Drumhead, or Brunswick Short Stem, *best*
     French ....**Caldwell** 1

Early Drumhead ....**Burt** 1

Early Large Schweinfurt.. ....**Calhoun** 1

Early Deep Red Erfurt............................**Calumet**.... 2

       LATE, OR AUTUMN AND WINTER SORTS.

Mammoth Rock Red.   This is by far the largest and surest
heading of the red Cabbages, and makes heads as solid as any in
cultivation. Color deepest blood red. Should be planted largely,
as it is the best· ....**Cambria**..... 4

Large Red Drumhead, *for pickling*. ....**Camden**..... 1

Stone Mason Marblehead............................**Camp**. 1

Louisville Drumhead, *true*. . ... **Cass** 1

Late Flat Dutch, *best French*...... ....**Cannon**......

Late Flat Dutch, *American*........................ ...**Carbon** 1

D. M. Ferry & Co's Premium Flat Dutch........**Carlton**...... 1

Large Drumhead, *best French*.............. ....**Caroline**.....

Large Drumhead, *American*........ ....**Carson** 1

D. M. Ferry & Co's Premium Drumhead........**Carver**. 1

Bridgeport Late Drumhead ....**Cascade**..... 1

Marblehead Mammoth Drumhead................**Casey**........ 1

Green Glazed.......................................**Cayuga**.... . 1

Savoy, Early Dwarf Ulm.. ....**Chaffee** 1

Savoy, Improved American, *extra*.................**Chariton** ... 1

Savoy, Drumhead......... ....**Charlotte** ... 1

CARROT—

Earliest Short Horn, *for forcing*....................**Chase**.. ....

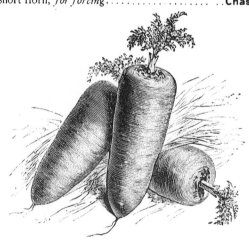

DANVERS.

CARROT—Continued.

	Tel. Cipher.	Per Lb.
Early Scarlet Horn	Chattooga	$0 60
Early Half Long Scarlet Carentan, *coreless*	Chautauqua	55
Half Long Scarlet Nantes, Stump Rooted	Cheshire	50
Chantenay, *stump-rooted, very productive*	Cherokee	50

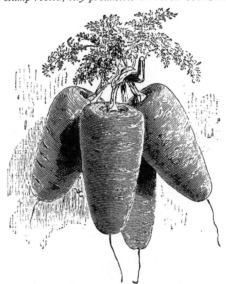

CHANTENAY CARROT.

The roots are usable so young that this variety is forced under glass largely in some localities' while it grows large and keeps as well as the Danvers or Long Orange.

	Tel. Cipher.	Per Lb.
Early Half Long Scarlet, Stump Rooted	Chemung	45
Danvers	Chehalis	45
Guerande, or Ox Heart	Chicot	65
Long Orange, *improved, best stock*	Chisago	50
Large White Vosges	Chilton	45
D. M. Ferry & Co's Improved Short White	Choteau	45
Large White Belgian	Choctaw	35

CAULIFLOWER—Our stock of Cauliflower will be found to be of the finest quality. We sell no Italian grown seed

	Tel. Cipher.	Per. Oz.	Per Lb.
Ferry's Early Puritan	Clare	$2 50	$30 00
Early Snowball. *Our stock is unsurpassed*	Clallam	2 00	25 00
Extra Early Dwarf Erfurt, *finest strain*	Claiborne	1 75	20 00
Extra Early Paris	Clatsop	80	8 00
Early Erfurt	Chowan	1 00	10 00
Early London	Clarion	30	3 00
Early Paris, or Nonpariel	Clarke	45	4 50
LeNormand's Short Stem, *true*	Clayton	75	6 50
Large Algiers	Cleveland	65	6 50
Veitch's Autumn Giant	Cloud	40	4 00

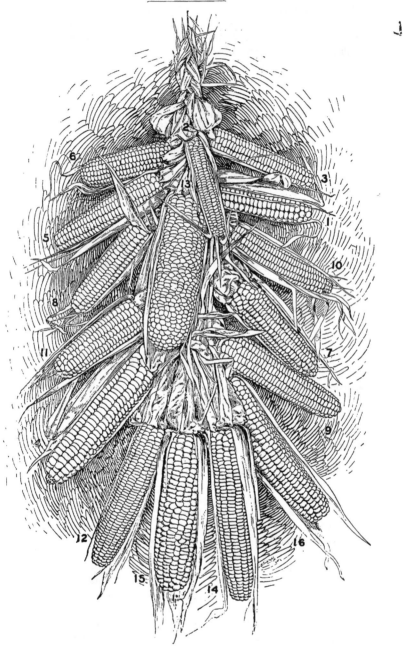

CELERY—

	Tel. Cipher.	Per Lb.
Golden Yellow, Large Solid, *self-blanching*	Cobb	$2 50
White Plume, *finest strain*	Cochise	2 00
Perfection Heartwell	Cochran	1 00
Golden Heart, or Golden Dwarf	Cooke	75
Giant Pascal	Coahoma	1 25
Dwarf White Solid	Cole	75
Crawford's Half Dwarf	Colbert	1 00
Boston Market	Collin	1 00
Seymour's White Solid	Colquitt	75
Incomparable Dwarf Crimson, *a fine sort*	Colusa	1 00
Celeriac, or Turnip Rooted	Concho	75
Celeriac, Large Smooth Prague	Concordia	1 25
Celery Seed, *for flavoring*	Conejos	20

CHERVIL—

Curled	Comanche	75

CHICORY—

Large Rooted, or Coffee	Conway	40

COLLARDS—

Georgia Southern, or Creole, *selected stock*	Coos	50

CORN—CAUTION.—Sweet Corn in bulk, even after being thoroughly cured, will often gather moisture and spoil, particularly if it has been exposed to a low temperature. To prevent this it should be taken out of the bags as soon as received and spread in a dry place. **Our quotations are per measured bushel, shelled** D. M. F. & CO.

☞Figures at left of Varieties correspond to figures on cut.

SWEET, OR SUGAR VARIETIES. Per Bu.

1	**Cory,** *very early*	Copiah	2 50
	White Cob Cory. We have been working on this variety for three years, selecting carefully to the White Cob type, and have succeeded in fixing the type so that a large proportion of them come true. We now offer it, without hesitation, as the best extra early Corn for market use. It differs in no way from ordinary Cory, except in the color of the cob and in having a lighter colored grain, having been obtained originally from it. It is fully as early, has as large ears, etc., and is in every way the best Corn for first early use	Coffey.	5 00
	Northern Pedigree, *extremely early*	Cowley	3 50
3	Early Minnesota, *very early*	Cottle	2 25
6	Crosby's Early	Crook	2 50
	Pee & Kay, *very early, with large ears*	Coshocton	2 50
4	Leet's Early, *large and early*	Cuming	2 50
7	Perry's Hybrid	Crenshaw	2 50
8	Early Sweet or Sugar	Curry	2 50
9	Moore's Early Concord	Custer	2 50
10	Black Mexican	Craig	2 50
12	Egyptian	Dade	Crop Failed.

CORN—Continued.

		Tel. Cipher.	· Per Bu.
14	Hickox Hybrid, *fine for canners* ....**Cuyahoga**		...$2 50
13	**Old Colony,** *large ears of the best quality, keeps long in condition for use, and is splendid for canners*.........**Dawson**		..... 2 75
15	Stowell's Evergreen... .... · ....**Dane**		.. .. 2 25
16	**Mammoth**................................. .....**Dallas**		.... 2 50

FIELD VARIETIES.

Extra Early Adams, *favorite in the South*........ ....**Dale**		.... 2 50
Early Adams, or Burlington............ .. ..**Darke**		...... 2 25
Early Red Blazed, *the hardiest*.................. . .....**Dixon**		.... 1 50
Early Golden Dent, or Pride of the North..............**Dickens**		..... 1 50
Early Golden Lenawee Dent ....**Dimmit**		..... 1 75
Rice, *for parching (bushel lots in ears)* ....**Donley**		..... 1 00

CORN SALAD, or Fetticus—

Per Lb.

Large Seeded, Large Leaved.................... .... **Dundy**....... 50

CRESS—

Curled, or Peppergrass......... ....**Dunn**........ 20
True Water........ ....**Duplin** 2 75

CUCUMBER—

Early Russian... ....**Duval**. 40

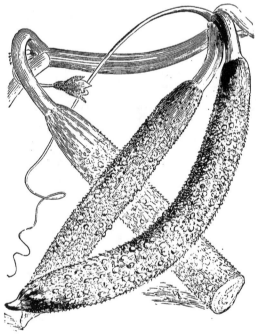

PARISIAN PROLIFIC PICKLING.

CUCUMBER—Continued.

	Tel. Cipher.	Per Lb.
Early Cluster.............................	Edwards.....	$0 45
Early Short Green, or Early Frame.	Edgar........	50
Chicago, or Westerfield Pickling, *one of the best*...	Effingham...	50
Jersey Pickling....................	Emery...	Crop Failed.
D. M. Ferry & Co's Perfection Pickling..........	Erie.........	75
Boston Pickling, or Green Prolific..............	Encinal......	50
Parisian Prolific Pickling......................	Ellsworth ...	1 00
Nichol's Medium Green..........................	Erath........	50
Early White Spine, *excellent for forcing*....	Eaton.......	45
Arlington..	Echols.......	50
Bismarck, Long White	Elbert.......	50
Improved Long Green...............	Elko...	50
Small Gherkins, *for pickles*............................	Estill........	75

EGG PLANT—

	Tel. Cipher.	Per Oz.	Per Lb.
Early Long Purple............................	Eureka......	$ 15	$1 25
Black Pekin, *extra early and very large*......	Falls........	40	4 00
Large New York Purple.................	Faulk.......	40	4 00
D. M. Ferry & Co's Improved Purple, *extra large, the leading market sort*............	Fayette......	45	4 50

D. M. FERRY & CO'S IMPROVED PURPLE.   BLACK PEKIN.

ENDIVE—

		Per Lb.
Green Curled.................................	Fisher.......	1 00
Ever White Curled.........	Florence....	1 25
Broad Leaved Batavian...	Floyd........	1 00
GARLIC Bulbs..................	Foote........	20
HORSE RADISH, Small Roots, per 100, 75c..	Foster.......	

KALE, or Borecole— Tel. Cipher.   Per Lb.

    German Dwarf Green, Extra Curled..............Frontier. ...$0 75

    German Dwarf Purple...... ....Fulton....... 75

    German Dwarf Green, or German Greens..............Frio...... .. 35

    Half Dwarf Moss Curled ....Furnas 75

    Tall Green Curled Scotch.... ....Fresno....... 75

KOHL RABI—

    Early White Vienna, *extra for forcing*.... ....Gaines 1 50

    Early Purple Vienna, *extra for forcing*.. ....Garland 1 50

    Large Green.................................Gallia 90

LEEK—

    London Flag..... ....Garza 1 50

LETTUCE—

    Early Tennis Ball, *s. b.*.. ....Gaston....... 50

    Tilton's White Star, *s. w.*.............Graham..... 1 50

    Black Seeded Simpson, *always reliable*..............Geneva..... 60

    Buttercup, *early, s. w* ....Gates.. 60

    Simpson's Early Curled, *s. w*......................Genesee ... 50

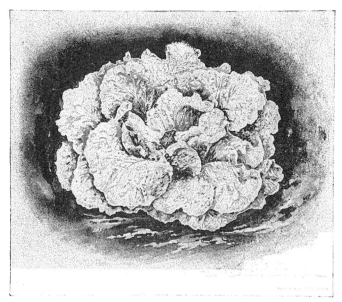

TILTON'S WHITE STAR LETTUCE.

A white seeded Lettuce, having enormously large, loose heads, after the style of Black Seeded Simpson. The leaves are larger, thicker, darker colored, and stand longer without wilting. Planted in the open ground it does not run to seed so quickly. Splendid for forcing or early planting outdoors, and for shipping long distances. **Per lb., $1.50.**

LETTUCE—Continued.

	Tel. Cipher.	Per Lb.
Hubbard's Market, *s. w*	Goodhue ...	$0 60
Early Boston Curled, *s. b.*	Gibson	50
Ferry's Early Prize Head, *s. w , best for family use...*	Gingras......	50
Hanson, *s. w., heads large, very solid.*...............	Glynn.. ....,	50
Early Curled Silesia, *s. w.*.....	Grove..	50
Grand Rapids, *s. b., extra good for forcing.*.......	Grant..	1 00

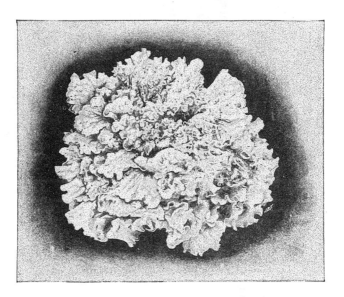

GRAND RAPIDS LETTUCE.

An upright growing, rapid maturing variety, unexcelled for close planting under glass. So remarkably slow to wilt after cutting as to make it one of the very best for growing to ship long distances. **Per lb., $1.00.**

Frankfort Head, *s. b*..............	Gosper......	50
Large Drumhead, or Victoria Cabbage, *s. w*...........	Gove	50
Philadelphia Butter, or Early White Head, *s. w.*	Gilmer......	50
Deacon, *s. w., compact and of superb quality.*...........	Gilpin........	60
Brown Dutch, *s. b., very hardy.*...................	Greeley......	60
Early White Self=Folding Cos, *s. w*........	Grenada.....	90

MARTYNIA—

Pickling.................................	Gregg	2 00

MELON, MUSK—

Jenny Lind.	Hamilton....	45
Extra Early Citron.........	Hamlin......	40
Baltimore, or Acme, *earliest first-class melon*.......	Hardy........	35
Skillman's Fine Netted	Hampton....	35

MELON, MUSK—Continued.   Tel. Cipher.   Per Lb.

Small Green Nutmeg...................... ....Hardin......$0 35
Early White Japan............................ .... Hardeman ..   35
Improved Large Green Nutmeg ....Harlan.......   50
Pine Apple....... ....Harper.. ...   35

HACKENSACK.

EMERALD GEM.

Hackensack, *early and of large size.......* ....Harris.......   50
Montreal, *true, very large and desirable............* ...Harnett......   45
Bay View...Grundy......   35
Casaba, or Green Persian........................ ....Hart....   35
Osage, or Improved Miller's Cream, *popular.....* Gwinnett....   45
Emerald Gem...................................Guthrie......   50

OSAGE.

JAPAN CORAL FLESH.

Surprise, *our stock is unequaled..* ....Grimes......   40
Japan Coral Fleshed, *prolific; good quality.........* .Gunnison....   35
Long Yellow..... ....Hawkins.....   35

KOLB'S GEM—The Most Popular Melon with Shippers.

MELON, WATER—

	Tel. Cipher.	Per Lb.
Phinney's Early	Hendricks	$0 30
D. M. Ferry & Co's Peerless, *best for home market*	Hill	30

Thomas & Huyette, Eng. Detroit.

DIXIE--A New and Valuable Variety.

MELON, WATER—Continued.

	Tel. Cipher.	Per Lb.
Boss	Hemphill	$0 80
Black Spanish	Henrico	25
Gypsy, or Georgia Rattlesnake	**Hinds**	80
Cuban Queen	Hays	80
Kolb's Gem, *best shipper*	**Haywood**	80
Dixie, *new, splendid shipper*	**Hennepin**	45
Mammoth Iron Clad	Hitchcock	80
Dark Icing, or Ice Rind, *fine quality*	Highland	80
Long Light Icing	Hickory	80
Round Light Icing	Hillsdale	80
Mountain Sweet, *extra good*	**Hernando**	25
Mountain Sprout	**Hertford**	80
Orange, *flesh separates easily from rind*	Hickman	60
Ice Cream, *true white seeded*	Hidalgo	80
Citron, *for preserving*	Hinsdale	80

MUSHROOM SPAWN—

English	Hocking	10
French	3 lb. boxes, $1.00 Hockley	

MUSTARD—

Golden, *fine flavor, very beautiful*	**Holt**	50
White English	Holmes	12
Southern Giant Curled	**Hood**	40

NASTURTIUM—

Tall Mixed	Holly	50

OKRA—

White Velvet, *the best*	**Houghton**	80
Dwarf White	Houston	25

ONION—*All prime new stock, and mostly our own growth, on our own Greenfield Seed Farms.*

Extra Early Red	Howard	1 15
Extra Early Red, *extra, our own growth*	**Howell**	1 40
Southport Red Globe	Hughes	1 15
Southport Red Globe, *extra, our own growth*	**Humbolt**	1 40
Large Red Wethersfield	Huron	1 15
Large Red Wethersfield, *extra, our own growth*	**Hyde**	1 25
Large Yellow Dutch, or Strasburg	Ida	1 25
Yellow Danvers	Iberia	1 25
Yellow Globe Danvers	Idaho	1 40
Yellow Globe Danvers, *extra, our own growth*	**Ingham**	1 50
Michigan Yellow Globe, *our own growth*	**Inyo**	2 00
White Portugal (*American Silverskin*)	Iosco Crop Failed.	
White Globe	**Iredell**	2 25
El Paso, or Large Mexican	Iroquois	2 25

MICHIGAN YELLOW GLOBE.

Through unavoidable circumstances we were unable to offer seed of this splendid variety in any quantity last season, but this year we are fairly well supplied with a fine stock grown on our own Greenfield Seed Farms.

WE SPEAK ADVISEDLY WHEN WE SAY THIS IS THE

FINEST SHAPED, BEST COLORED AND LARGEST CROPPER

OF ANY OF THE YELLOW GLOBE ONIONS.

Our own large plantings for seed and the fields we have seen growing for market have fully demonstrated this. Wherever we have sold it, either in large or small quantities, it has given unbounded satisfaction, and we cannot **urge you too strongly to plant largely of it for this year's crop.**

ONION—Continued.

Tel. Cipher.   Per Lb.

IMPORTED VARIETIES.

Round White Silverskin, *for pickling* ....**Isabella** $1 50
White Silverskin, *for bunching* ....:.............**Island** 1 25
Early Neapolitan Marzajola, *fine white Silverskin sort* ....**Itasca** 1 50

No. 1, Extra Early Red; No. 2, Large Red Wethersfield; No. 3, Yellow Danvers; No. 4, White Portugal; No. 5, White Silverskin; No. 6, White Globe.

Mammoth Silver King ....**Iberville** 1 75
Giant Rocca.................................**Isanti** 1 50
Giant White Italian Tripoli....................**Izard** 1 50
Queen, *true, for pickling* ....**Jackson** 1 50

PARSLEY—

Plain... ....**Juab** 25
Carter's Fern Leaved.... ....**Kanawha** ... 60
Champion Moss Curled......................**Kankakee** ... 60
Fine Triple Curled, or Myatt's Garnishing.......**Karnes** 55
Turnip Rooted, or Hamburg.... ... .**Kaufman**..... 40

PARSNIP—

	Tel Cipher.	Per Lb.
Long White Dutch, or Sugar....	Juniata......$0	20
Hollow Crown, or Guernsey.	**Kalkaska....**	20

GUERNSEY PARSNIP.   PREMIUM GEM.

PEAS—*All smooth Peas, 60 lbs. per bu.; all wrinkled Peas, 56 lbs. per bu. Wrinkled varieties marked thus.**

EXTRA EARLY SORTS.

		Per Bu.
Ferry's First and Best, *finest strain, extra selected....* **Kearney..**	..	2 75
D. M. Ferry & Co's Extra Early, *equal to any offered* *in sealed bags........ ....* **Kenton......**		2 75
Improved Early Daniel O'Rourke...................... **Kearns...**	..	2 75
***Bliss' American Wonder,** true........ ....* **Kenosha....**		4 00
Earliest of All, or Alaska, *the finest blue, extra early* *smooth Pea. As early as First and Best..........* **Kewaunee...**		3 50
Kentish Invicta, *true.............................* **Kinney......**		2 75
*Laxton's Alpha, *finest quality................* **Kimble......**		2 75
Ferry's Extra Early Tom Thumb................ **Kiowa.......**		3 50
Blue Peter, or Blue Tom Thumb.................... **Knox........**		3 50

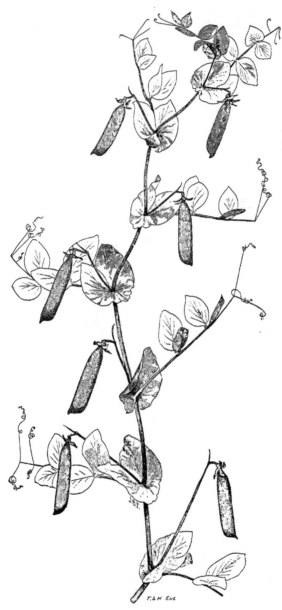

EARLIEST OF ALL, OR ALASKA.

PEAS—Continued.
EARLY SORTS.

<table>
<thead>
<tr><th></th><th>Tel. Cipher.</th><th>Per Bu.</th></tr>
</thead>
<tbody>
<tr><td>*McLean's Little Gem</td><td>Kossuth</td><td>$3 00</td></tr>
<tr><td>*Premium Gem</td><td>Labette</td><td>3 00</td></tr>
<tr><td>*Bliss' Ever Bearing</td><td>Laclede</td><td>2 75</td></tr>
<tr><td>Extra Early Kent, true</td><td>Lamoille</td><td>2 50</td></tr>
<tr><td>*McLean's Advancer, favorite for market</td><td>Laurel</td><td>3 00</td></tr>
</tbody>
</table>

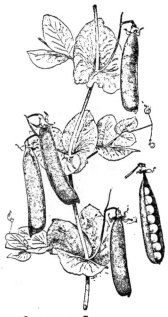

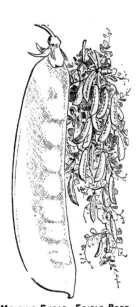

CHAMPION OF ENGLAND.   MELTING SUGAR, EDIBLE PODS.

<table>
<tbody>
<tr><td>*Telephone, very popular, extra choice stock</td><td>Lamar</td><td>3 50</td></tr>
<tr><td>*Bliss' Abundance</td><td>Lavaca</td><td>2 75</td></tr>
</tbody>
</table>

LATE SORTS.

<table>
<tbody>
<tr><td>*Yorkshire Hero</td><td>Laurens</td><td>2 60</td></tr>
<tr><td>*Champion of England, choice</td><td>Lehigh</td><td>2 25</td></tr>
<tr><td>*Stratagem</td><td>Lenawee</td><td>4 00</td></tr>
<tr><td>*Pride of the Market</td><td>Lenoir</td><td>4 00</td></tr>
<tr><td>Large Blue Imperial, choice</td><td>Leon</td><td>2 50</td></tr>
<tr><td>Large White Marrowfat, hand-picked</td><td>Lewis</td><td>1 75</td></tr>
<tr><td>Large White Marrowfat</td><td>Liberty</td><td>1 50</td></tr>
<tr><td>Large Black Eye Marrowfat, hand-picked</td><td>Licking</td><td>1 75</td></tr>
<tr><td>Large Black Eye Marrowfat</td><td>Lincoln</td><td>1 50</td></tr>
<tr><td>Dwarf Sugar, Edible Pods, gray seeds</td><td>Linn</td><td>4 50</td></tr>
<tr><td>Melting Sugar, Edible Pods, New. By far the largest cropper and having the largest, smoothest, most tender pods of the best flavor of any of this class</td><td>Levy</td><td>6 00</td></tr>
<tr><td>Tall Sugar, Edible Pods, gray seeds</td><td>Leano</td><td>4 50</td></tr>
</tbody>
</table>

PEAS—Continued.

FIELD SORTS.

	Tel. Cipher.	Per Bu.
Common White............................	Lucas	Market Price.
No. 1 White........................	Macon.	"
Golden Vine........................	Macomb ...	"
Common Blue..	Lynn.	
Blue Prussian.......................	Magoffin	"

PEPPER—

	Tel. Cipher.	Per Lb.
Red Chili..........................	Mahaska ...	$2 00
Cardinal, *very handsome*......	Malheur.....	2 50
Long Red Cayenne.....................	Manatee....	1 50

GOLDEN DAWN.   LARGE BELL, OR BULL NOSE.

Large Squash..................	Maricopa....	1 50
Large Bell, or Bull Nose..	Marion....	1 50
Sweet Mountain...................	Mariposa....	1 50
Golden Dawn,......	Marquette..	1 50
Ruby King....	Massac......	2 00

PUMPKIN—

Large Yellow...............Per bu., $2 25 ..	Mobile......	15
Cushaw.	Mohave......	40
Sweet Cheese, or Kentucky Field, Per bu., $4.00 ..	Mono........	25

LARGE YELLOW PUMPKIN.

SWEET CHEESE, OR KENTUCKY FIELD PUMPKIN.

RADISH—*All our Radish Seeds are the very finest French grown stock.*

Tel. Cipher.   Per Lb.

Non Plus Ultra, or Early Deep Scarlet Turnip, Forcing, *the Earliest, fine for forcing* . . . . **Moody** $0 45

Early Scarlet, Turnip Rooted . . . . **Mora** 25

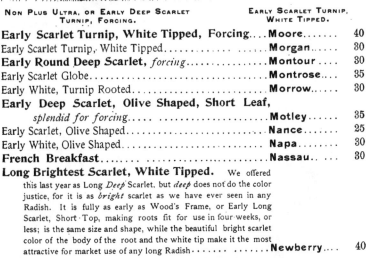

NON PLUS ULTRA, OR EARLY DEEP SCARLET TURNIP, FORCING.

EARLY SCARLET TURNIP, WHITE TIPPED.

Early Scarlet Turnip, White Tipped, Forcing . . . . **Moore** 40

Early Scarlet Turnip, White Tipped . . . . **Morgan** 30

Early Round Deep Scarlet, *forcing* . . . . **Montour** 30

Early Scarlet Globe . . . . **Montrose** 35

Early White, Turnip Rooted . . . . **Morrow** 30

Early Deep Scarlet, Olive Shaped, Short Leaf, *splendid for forcing* . . . . **Motley** 35

Early Scarlet, Olive Shaped . . . . **Nance** 25

Early White, Olive Shaped . . . . **Napa** 30

French Breakfast . . . . **Nassau** 30

Long Brightest Scarlet, White Tipped.   We offered this last year as Long *Deep* Scarlet, but *deep* does not do the color justice, for it is as *bright* scarlet as we have ever seen in any Radish. It is fully as early as Wood's Frame, or Early Long Scarlet, Short · Top, making roots fit for use in four weeks, or less; is the same size and shape, while the beautiful bright scarlet color of the body of the root and the white tip make it the most attractive for market use of any long Radish · · · · · · · · · · · · · · · **Newberry** 40

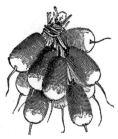

FRENCH BREAKFAST.

EARLY SCARLET TURNIP, WHITE TIPPED, FORCING.

RADISH—Continued.

	Tel. Cipher.	Per Lb.
Early Long Scarlet, Short Top, *improved*	Monona	$0 25
Wood's Early Frame	Montague	30
Improved Chartier	Montcalm	30
Long White Vienna, or Lady Finger	Morehouse	35
Long White Naples	Nelson	30
Early White Giant Stuttgart	Nemaha	35
White Strasburg	Navajo	35
Large White Summer Turnip	Navarro	35
Golden Globe	Morton	30
Gray Summer, Turnip Rooted	Murray	30

WINTER VARIETIES.

Scarlet China	Neshoba	35
California Mammoth White China	Niagara	30
Large White Spanish	Newton	30
Round Black Spanish	Ness	35
Long Black Spanish	Newport	35

RAPE—

Dwarf Essex	Nobles	15

RHUBARB, or Pie Plant—

Victoria,	Nodaway	1 00
Giant	Norton	1 00
Linnæus	Noxubee	1 00
Rhubarb Roots....Per doz., $1.25	Nueces	

SALSIFY, or Vegetable Oyster—

Large White	Oakland	60
Mammoth Sandwich Island	Obion	75

SALSIFY.

SPINAGE—LONG STANDING PRICKLY.

	Tel. Cipher.	Per
SPINAGE—		
Savoy Leaved	Oconto......	$0
Round Summer.................	Ocean......	
Improved Thick Leaved.......	Oconee.....	
Long Standing, *dark green, thick leaved*...........	Ogemaw....	
Prickly Winter.................	Ogle........	
Long Standing Prickly, *new, very superior*......	Ohio....	
SQUASH, Summer—		
Early Yellow Bush Scallop.....	Olmstead ...	
Early White Bush Scallop	Oneida.....	
Summer Crookneck............	Onslow......	
Mammoth Summer Crookneck, *new*............	Orange	3
Perfect Gem.................	Oldham.. ...	

AUTUMN OR WINTER SORTS.

Early Prolific Orange Marrow, *new.* ....Oliver.........

BOSTON MARROW.

Improved American Turban, (Essex Hybrid) ....Ontario.. ...
Boston Marrow, *our own extra select stock*.. ....Oscoda.......
Hubbard, *our own extra select stock* ....Otoe.........

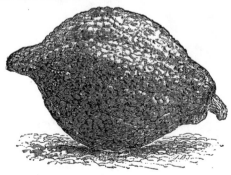

HUBBARD.

SQUASH—Continued.

Tel. Cipher.

Butman................ ....-...........Osborne....
Marblehead.......... ....Ormsby....
Winter Crookneck.................... ... .Oswego.....

SUGAR CANE—

Early Amber... ....$3.00 per bu. of 50 lbs..Otsego ....
Early Orange.... ....$3.00 per bu. of 50 lbs..Otter.......

SUNFLOWER—

Large Russian......... ....$1.50 per bu..Ottawa.....

TOBACCO—

Sterling .... Per oz., 15c..Ochiltree....
Lacks............................... " 15c..Orleans.....
Hester ·. ....·. .. ... " 15c..Overton..
Sweet Oronoco.......... .... " 15c..Owen.......
Bradley Broad Leaf......... .. .. " 15c..Owsley... .
Persian Rose........................... " 15c..Oxford .....
Big Havana........ .... " 15c..Ozaukee....
Connecticut Seed Leaf..... ....Ouray.......
Havana.... ....Ozark ......

TOMATO—*All our tomato seeds are grown from stocks raised strictly for seed purposes and from seed stocks, carefully selected and saved by ourselves, and we challenge comparison of our stocks with any offered by anyone.*

Atlantic Prize..... ....Pitkin......

ONE-THIRD NATURAL SIZE.

ATLANTIC PRIZE TOMATO.

The earliest tomato grown. Beyond all doubt the largest, smoothest, and in every v best extra early tomato. The most careful tests have failed to reveal any difference betwe and Early Ruby, except that our stock of Atlantic Prize has been more carefully selected.

EARLY MICHIGAN, OR EARLY RED APPLE.

We have changed the name of this splendid variety, because many of our customers, naturally enough, confuse it with the White Apple, taking it to be its counterpart except in color, whereas it has medium sized to large fruits which are as smooth, solid and free from core, and of as fine flavor as any tomato grown. It ripens its first fruits almost as early as any variety, and continues in full bearing until cut off by frost. For general market, canners' or family use, there is no variety which will be more uniformly satisfactory. Our stock has been selected with the greatest care for many years.

TOMATO—Continued.

	Tel. Cipher.	Per Lb.
Early Michigan, or Early Red Apple, *new*	Page	$1 75
D. M. Ferry & Co's Optimus. *The handsomest and best. Our own original selected stock*	Pawnee	1 25
Early Conqueror	Pacific	1 25
Canada Victor	Perry	1 25
Livingston's Favorite	Palo	1 25
Trophy, *true, extra selected*	Pickett	1 50
Paragon	Person	1 25

Ignotum. We have selected our stock of this with the greatest care, and think it is free from all tendency to produce small, inferior fruits. There is much inferior stock of this variety in the market .... **Pleasants** ... 2 00

TOMATO—Continued.

	Tel. Cipher.	Per Lb.
Livingston's Perfection	Pamlico	$1 25
Acme, *extra selected.*	Phelps	1 25
Essex Early Hybrid, *earliest purple sort.*	Paulding	1 25
Dwarf Champion.	Polk	1 50

IGNOTUM.

Livingston's Beauty.	Pecos	1 25
Cincinnati Purple, *very large*	Passaic	1 50
Mikado, or Turner's Hybrid	Potter	2 00
Peach.	Pickaway	1 75
Golden Queen	Pembina	2 00

ACME.   LIVINGSTON'S BEAUTY.

White Apple	Pickens	2 50
Red Pear Shaped	Peoria	1 75
Yellow Plum	Pepin	1 75
Red Cherry	Phillips	1 75
Yellow Cherry	Pettis	1 75
Husk Tomato, or Ground Cherry	Piatt	2 00

TURNIP—	WHITE FLESHED SORTS.	Tel. Cipher.	Per Lb.
Extra Early Purple Top Milan, *strap leaved*		Pinal	$0 30
White Egg		Portage	25
Early White Flat Dutch, Strap Leaved		Powhatan	20

EXTRA EARLY PURPLE TOP MILAN.

Early Purple Top, Strap Leaved, *improved*	Presidio	20
Purple Top White Globe	Raleigh	20
Cow Horn, or Long White	Preston	25

WHITE EGG.   **PURPLE TOP WHITE GLOBE.**

Large White Norfolk	Pulaski	18
Large Red Top Norfolk	Putnam	18
Pomeranian White Globe	Quitman	18
Sweet German, *true*	Ramsey	25
Seven Top, *for turnip greens*	Randall	20
YELLOW FLESHED SORTS.		
Large Amber Globe	Renville	25
Orange Jelly, or Robertson's Golden Ball	Rawlins	20
Purple Top Yellow Aberdeen	Refugio	25

TURNIP—Continued. Tel. Cipher.
RUTA BAGAS OR SWEDES.

Monarch, or Tankard, *new, extra*.. ....**Rains**.....

Yellow Swede, or Ruta Baga............. .. ..**Rhea**....

Carter's Imperial Purple Top Ruta Baga.... ....**Rich**......

**D. M. Ferry & Co's Improved Purple Top Yellow
Ruta Baga**............................ .... ..**Riley**....

Laing's Purple Top Ruta Baga................**Rockland**.

MONARCH, OR TANKARD.

Sutton's Champion Ruta Baga........................**Ringgold**

Drummond's Ruta Baga.... ....**Russell**..

Shepherd's Golden Globe Ruta Baga....... ....**Rinehart**

Bangholm Swede................................**Ritchie**..

Sweet Russian, or White Ruta Baga....................**Roone**...

SWEET HERBS—

Anise............. ....**Roberts**..

Balm............................ ....**Robeson**

Basil, Sweet ....**Rolette**..

Bene........................ ....**Roop** ...

Borage .. ..**Routt**....

Caraway, for Sowing....... ....**Rowan**...

Caraway, for Flavoring..... ....**Rush** ..

Catnip.............. .. ..**Rutland**..

SWEET HERBS—Continued.

	Tel. Cipher.	Per Lb.
Coriander, for Sowing	Saginaw	$0 40 35
Coriander, for Flavoring	Salem	25
Dandelion, Improved Thick Leaved	Saline	3 50 4 00
Dill	Sampson	40
Fennel, Sweet	Sanilac	50
Horehound	Saratoga	1 50
Hyssop	Sarpy	1 25
Lavender	Saunders	75
Marjoram, Sweet	Schley	1 00
Rosemary	Scott	3 00
Rue	Screven	1 00
Saffron	Searcy	75
Sage, Broad Leaf	Seneca	1 25
Savory, Summer	Sevier	50
Tansy	Seward	2 00
Thyme, English	Shannon	2 75 2 5
Wormwood	Sharkey	1 50

FRUIT SEEDS—

	Tel. Cipher.	Per Lb.
Apple Seeds ....per bu., $6.00	Shasta	30
Cherry Stones, *Mahaleb*	Shawnee	30
Cherry Stones, *Mazzard*	Shelby	20
Pear Seed	Sheyenne	1 25
Plum Stones	Sierra	20
Quince Seed	Sioux	1 75

FOREST TREE AND HEDGE SEEDS—

EVERGREEN.

	Tel. Cipher.	Per Lb.
Arbor Vitæ, American, (*Thuja occidentalis*)	Skamania	2 00
Fir, Silver (*Abies pectinata*)	Socorro	75
Hemlock (*Tsuga Canadensis*)	Solano	3 00
Pine, Scotch (*Pinus sylvestris*)	Spink	1 50
Pine, Weymouth, or White (*Pinus strobus*)	Spalding	1 75
Spruce, Norway (*Abies Excelsa*)	Spokane	1 00

DECIDUOUS.

	Tel. Cipher.	Per Lb.
Ash, White (*Fraxinus Americana*)	Simpson	40
Ash, European (*Fraxinus excelsior*)	Siskiyou	50
Birch, White (*Betula alba*)	Snohomish	50
Box Elder	Sedgwick	40
Catalpa, Hardy (*Catalpa speciosa*)	Sonoma	50
Larch (*Larix Europœa*)	Somervell	75
Linden, European (*Tilia Europœa*)	Spencer	60
Locust, Honey (*Gleditschia triacanthos*)	Sisseton	25
Locust, Yellow (*Robinia pseudo-acacia*)	Snyder	25
Mulberry, White (*Morus alba*)	Sperry	1 50
Mulberry, Russian	Spartanburg	1 25
Osage Orange (*Maclura aurantiaca*). $6.00 per bu. of 33 lbs	Stanley	35

BIRD SEEDS—

Tel. Cipher. · Per I

Canary	Stanton	$0
Hemp	Starke	
Rape	Stearns	
Maw	Steele	
Millet	Steuben	
Lettuce	Stewart	
Cuttle Bone	Stokes	
Mixed Bird Seed	Storey	

CLOVER—

Per I

Mammoth, or Large Red	Suffolk	Marl Pric	
Medium Red, or June	Sulley	"	

Per I

Alsike, or Swedish ....$10.00 per bu..	Sumter		
Bokhara Sweet Clover (*Melilotus alba*)	Sussex		
Crimson Trefoil, or Scarlet Italian.	Surrey		
White Dutch... .....$10.00 per bu..	Sutter		
Lucern, or Alfalfa $6.00 "	Swain		

GRASS SEEDS—

Per I

Timothy	Swift	Marl Pric
Orchard Grass (sack lots, about 8 bu., $1.40 per bu.)	Talbot	1
Red Top (sack lots, about 5 bu., 50c. per bu.)	Talladega	
Red Top, Fancy, *cleaned from chaff*, (per 100 lbs., $8.00; per lb., 12c.).	Tallapoosa	
Fowl Meadow, or False Red Top	Tama	3
Blue Grass, Kentucky, *fancy clean*, (sack lots, about 8 bu. $2.40 per bu)	Tate	2
Johnson Grass	Tipton	2
Perennial Rye Grass (sack lots, about 6 bu., $1.25 per bu)	Taylor	1
Meadow Fescue, or English Blue Grass	Tazewell	2
Sweet Vernal Grass Per lb., 20c..	Tensas	1
Hungarian Grass	Terrell	Mar Pric
Millet, Common	Thayer	'
Millet, German	Tioga	'
Fine Mixed Lawn	Titus	2
Extra Fine Mixed, Central Park Mixture	Traile	3

MISCELLANEOUS SEEDS—

Barley, Common	Upson	1
Barley, Naked or Hulless	Vigo	3
Rye, Fall or Winter	Wasco	1
Rye, Spring	Washington	1
Buckwheat, Common	Webb	1
Buckwheat, Silver Hull	Wharton	1
Buckwheat, Japanese, *new*	Whatcom	1
Flax Seed, for Sowing	Whitman	1
Hemp Seed, "	Wilkin	2
Spring Vetches, or Tares	Yuma	2
Wild Rice (*Zizania aquatica*)	Yuba	3

A SELECTED LIST

OF

FLOWER SEEDS IN BULK.

☞ We will not sell less than 1 oz. of sorts priced at 20c. per oz. or under; but we will put up ½ oz. of seeds priced at 25c. per oz. and over; ¼ oz. of seeds priced at 75c. per oz. and over; ⅛ oz. of seeds priced at $3 per oz. and over.

	PER OZ.	PER LB.
Adonis autumnalis.............................	$0 10	$0 50
Ageratum Mexicanum, blue......................	15	1 25
" Imperial Dwarf White..............	30	3 00
" Dwarf Blue (Tom Thumb)..........	30	3 00
Agrostemma coronaria..........................	15	1 25
" cœli rosa....	15	1 00
Alonsoa grandiflora..........	15	1 50
" Warszewiczii..........................	25	2 50

ALYSSUM, SWEET.

ASTER, DWARF CHRYSANTHEMUM.

	PER OZ.	PER LB.
Alyssum, Sweet, (Maritimum)....................	15	1 50
" Golden, (Saxatile).....................	25	2 50
Amaranthus melancholicus ruber...............	15	1 00
" tricolor, (Joseph's coat)...............	15	1 25
Aster, Dwarf Chrysanthemum, mixed.	1 50	
" " Pyramidal Bouquet, mixed	1 50	
" " German Quilled, mixed..	30	3 00
" " Imbricated Pompon, mixed...........	1 00	
" " Truffaut's Pæony Flowered Perfection, mixed.	1 50	
" " " " " crimson.....	2 00	
" " " " " light blue	2 00	
" " " " " snow white...	1 50	

	PER OZ.	PER LB.
Aster, Victoria, mixed............................	$2 00	
" " white, turning to azure blue......	2 50	
" Cocardeau, or Crown, mixed.......	1 50	
Bachelor's Button, Corn Flower, (Centaurea cyanus)........	10	75
Balloon Vine, (Cardiospermum halicacabum)......	15	1 00
Balsam Solferino, double...........	75	7 50
" Camellia Flowered, double, mixed......	50	5 00
" Pure White, "	75	
" Dwarf, mixed, "	40	4 00
" Tall, mixed, "	25	2 50

CANDYTUFT, ROCKET.   CANNA, CROZY'S HYBRIDS.

	PER OZ.	PER LB.
Bartonia aurea, yellow........................	15	1 00
Calliopsis, fine mixed	15	1 00
Canary Bird Flower, (Tropæolum canariense)......	40	4 00
Candytuft, (Odorata), fragrant white........	10	75
" White........................	10	50
" " Rocket........	15	1 25
" " " Selected to splendid large trusses; extra for cut flowers, known also as Empress Giant Snowflake, etc........	25	2 50
Purple........	15	1 50
" Fine, mixed, separate colors mixed......	15	1 00
Canna Indica, (Indian Shot)	15	1 00
" Crozy's finest hybrids, mixed........	50	5 00
Canterbury Bell, double mixed, (Campanula medium)......	40	
" " single " " "	15	1 50
Carnation, extra choice, double mixed......	3 00	
" double Vienna dwarf, mixed......	1 00	

	PER OZ.	PER LB.
Carnation, Picotee, extra fine double mixed... ¼ oz., $2.00..		
Castor Bean, (Ricinus sanguineus), red fruit.	$0 10	$0 50
" " gigantic, (Ricinus giganteus).	10	60
" " choice mixed	10	50
Catchfly, White, (Silene armeria alba)	10	60
" Red, (Silene armeria rubra).	10	60
" mixed..	10	50
Centaurea gymnocarpa..	50	
Chrysanthemum carinatum Burridgeanum, single..	15	1 25
" coronarium, double white..	15	1 00
" " yellow.	15	1 00
Cineraria hybrida, finest mixed... ⅛ oz., $6.00..		
" maritima. candidissima	30	
Clarkia, mixed..	15	1 25
Cobœa scandens.	60	

DAISY.

	PER OZ.	PER LB.
Cockscomb, dwarf, crimson..	75	
" " rose..	75	
" " yellow..	75	
" " finest mixed..	50	5 00
Columbine, (Aquilegia), double mixed..	15	1 25
Convolvulus minor, mixed, (Dwarf Morning Glory) ..	10	40
Cypress Vine, scarlet, (Ipomœa quamoclit)..	15	1 50
" " white, " ..	15	1 50
" " mixed, " ..	15	1 50
Dahlia, finest double mixed, from selected flowers.	2 00	
Daisy, double white, extra..	2 50	
" " red, (Longfellow), finest strain..	4 00	
" " mixed, finest quality.	2 50	
Datura Wrighti, (meteloides), pure white..	15	1 50
" chlorantha fl. pl., double yellow..	25	2 50
" fastuosa alba, double, pure white..	25	2 50
Eschscholtzia Californica, bright yellow, (California Poppy).	20	

	PER OZ.	PER LB.
Eschscholtzia crocea, double white, (California Poppy)	$0 75	
"　　　　" 　　striped, 　　　"	25	
"　　　mixed, finest colors, 　　"	20	
Euphorbia variegata	20	
Forget-me-not, blue, (Myosotis Alpestris)	50	
Four o'clock, gold striped, (Marvel of Peru)	10	40
"　　red, 　　　　"　　　　"	10	40
"　　white, 　　　　"　　　　"	10	40
"　　yellow, 　　　　"　　　　"	10	40
"　　white, red striped, "　　　"	10	40
"　　mixed, 　　　　"　　　　"	10	35
Fox Glove, splendid mixed, (Digitalis gloxinioides)	30	3 00
Gilia capitata, azure blue	10	50
" tricolor, three colored	10	50

GOURD, PEAR SHAPED.　　　　GOURD, BOTTLE.

Globe Amaranth, white, (Gomphrena globosa)		20
"　　"　　flesh colored, " 　　　　"		20
"　　"　　purple, 　　" 　　　　"		20
"　　"　　orange, 　　" 　　　"		30
"　　"　　striped, 　　" 　　　"		20
"　　"　　mixed, 　　" 　　　"		15
Godetia rubicunda splendens, lilac and purple		25
" roseo-alba, rose and white (Tom Thumb)		25
Gourd, Orange		20
" White, egg shaped		20
" Siphon, or dipper		20
" Hercules' club		20
" Apple shaped, striped		25
" Pear 　　" 　　ringed		20
" Bottle		20
" Powder Horn		20
" mixed		15
Helichrysum bracteatum, yellow		25
"　　monstrosum, largest double mixed		30
"　　compositum album, fl. pl.		40
Heliotrope, Dark Varieties mixed		1 00
Helipterum anthemoides		35
"　　Sanfordi		35

	PER OZ.	PER LB.
Hibiscus Africanus	$0 15	$1 00
Hollyhock, Double White, finest strain	1 50	
" " Canary Yellow, finest strain	1 50	
" " Rose, finest strain	2 00	
" ' Salmon, "	2 00	
" ' Crimson, "	2 00	
" " Choicest mixed	1 00	
" " mixed	50	
Honesty, or Satin Flower, (Lunaria biennis)	25	
Hyacinth Bean, Purple, (Dolichos lablab)	15	1 00
" " White, " "	15	1 00
" " mixed, " "	10	75

MOON FLOWER.

LARKSPUR, ROCKET.

		PER OZ.	PER LB.
Ipomœa coccinea, fine scarlet		20	
" bona nox, (good night), white		20	
" limbata, purple and white		20	
" " elegantissima, very large		25	
" (Calonyction) grandiflora, (Moon Flower), white seed		50	6 00
" " " " hybrid black seed		50	5 00
Job's Tears, (Coix lachryma)		10	50
Lantana, finest French hybrids, mixed		25	
Larkspur, (Delphinium), double dwarf rocket, mixed		15	1 25
" " elatum, Bee Larkspur, blue		25	
" " formosum, blue and white		50	
" " Chinese, white		30	

	PER OZ.	PER LB.
Linum grandiflorum rubrum, (Scarlet flax)...	$0 15	
Lobelia erinus gracilis, blue...	25	
Love Grove (Nemophila), mixed...	10	$0 40
Love-in-a-mist, (Nigella Damascena), double blue ...	10	60
" " " dwarf blue and white.	15	1 00
Lupin Hartwegi, blue...	10	60
" Cruikshanki, white, blue and yellow...	10	40
Lychnis Chalcedonica, (London Pride)...	20	
Lythrum roseum superbum...	25	

MIGNONETTE, MACHET.

	PER OZ.	PER LB.
Marigold, Meteor, (Calendula officinalis), double yellow...	15	1 00
" Prince of Orange, (Calendula officinalis), double orange...	15	1 00
" Tagetes signata pumila, yellow ...	25	2 50
" Cape (Calendula pongei), double white...	25	2 50
" " (Calendula pluvialis), single white...	15	1 00
Mesembryanthemum crystallinum (Ice Plant)...	20	2 00
Mignonette, Sweet, (Reseda odorata) ...	10	45
" Machet, (Reseda grandiflora)...	50	5 00
" Parson's White, (Reseda grandiflora)...	25	2 50
" Tall pyramidal, " "	15	1 25
" Bouquet dwarf, " "	35	
" Golden Queen, " "	30	
Mimulus moschatus, (Musk plant)...	3 00	
" tigrinus punctatus, (Monkey flower), finest spotted	1 25	
Momordica balsamina, (Balsam apple)...	20	2 00
" charantia, (Balsam pear)...	20	2 00
Morning Glory, (Convolvulus Major), mixed	10	30
Mourning Bride, Dwarf Mixed, (Scabiosa)...	20	
Nasturtium, Tall, (Tropæolum Lobbianum), Geant des Batailles	20	2 00
" " " Roi des Noirs	30	3 00
" " " Lucifer	30	3 00

				PER OZ.	PER LB.
Nasturtium, Tall, (Tropæolum Lobbianum), mixed..........				$0 15	$1 25
" (Tropæolum minor), dwarf,	Scarlet.............			10	
"	"	"	King Theodore.......	20	
"	"	"	Beauty............	10	
"	"	"	Yellow	10	
"	"	"	Pearl, white.........	15	
"	"	"	King of Tom Thumbs	20	
"	"	"	Spotted King........	10	
"	"	"	Empress of India......	25	
"	"	"	Crystal Palace Gem...	10	
"	"	"	mixed	10	50
Nolana, mixed.......................				15	
Pampas Grass, (Gynerium argenteum)...............				30	

PANSY, BUGNOT'S VERY LARGE STAINED.

Pansy, Emperor William...........................			75
"	King of the Blacks.......		75
"	Pure Yellow....		75
"	Variegated and striped...		1 00
"	Odier, or Large Stained, extra fine	¼ oz., $1.25	4 50
"	Bugnot's Superb Blotched.......	⅛ oz., $2.50	
"	Snow Queen, white........		75
"	Azure blue........		75
"	Gold margined.......		75

PE[

Pansy, Violet, white edged.. .. .. $0
   "   Trimardeau, very large flowered, mixed... 2
   "   Extra choice, mixed, large flowering. 1
   "   Fine mixed. ....
Peas, Everlasting, mixed, (Lathyrus latifolius)...............
Petunia hybrida, striped and blotched, choice mixed.........
   "   "   fine mixed..............
   "   "   large flowered, choicest mixed. 1-16 oz., $1.00..
   "   "   double, finest mixed ....1-16 oz., $2.50..
   "   "   double, fringed, mixed ....1-32 oz., $2.50..

PETUNIA, LARGE FLOWERED.

Phlox Drummondi, large flowered, extra choice mixed........
   "   "   "   "   white, our own growth, extra..
   "   "   "   "   scarlet.. ....
   "   "   "   "   Black Warrior......... .....
   "   "   "   "   alba oculata.............
   "   "   "   "   coccinea alba oculata......
   "   "   splendid mixed.............
Pink, China, double mixed, (Dianthus Chinensis)............
   "   "   Heddewigii, (Double Diadem). ....
   "   "   "   finest single mixed ....
Poppy, Carnation, double white ....
   "   "   "   mixed...... ....
Portulaca, single, large flowered, pure white.......
   "   "   "   "   yellow.............
   "   "   "   "   "   striped.....
   "   "   "   "   caryophylloides, Carnation striped..
   "   "   "   "   splendid mixed...
   "   double, "   "   "   3
Primrose, Evening, (Œnothera acaulis alba)......
   "   "   "   Lamarckiana).............
Primula Sinensis fimbriata, choicest mixed...... .....1/8 oz., $4.00.. 25

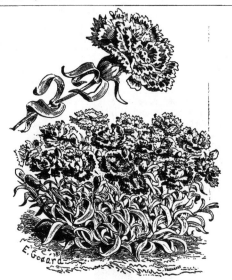

PINK, DOUBLE CHINA.

	PER OZ.	PER LB.
Pyrethrum aureum, Golden Feather............	$0 60	
" " selaginoides, new, extra	2 00	
" roseum...............................	50	$5 00
Rhodanthe, mixed....... ..	50	
Salpiglossis, finest hybrids, mixed...............	35	
Sensitive Plant, (Mimosa pudica)................	50	

SUN FLOWER. DOUBLE.

SALPIGLOSSIS.

	PER OZ.	PER LB.
Smilax, (Myrsiphyllum asparagoides)....	1 00	10 00
Snapdragon, (Antirrhinum), finest mixed........	25	
Solanum pseudo-capsicum............	30	
Stock, double, (German Ten Weeks), extra fine mixed	75	
" " " " large flowering, mixed...	1 25	
Sun Flower, (Helianthus Californicus), double...	10	75

	PER OZ.	PER LB.
Sweet Peas, Miss Blanche Ferry..............	$0 15	$1 50
" " Indigo King.	30	3 00
" " Invincible Scarlet..............	15	1 50
" " " White	30	3 00
" " Boreatton, maroon, splendid....	30	3 00
" " Striped....................	15	1 50
" " Adonis, Carmine Rose	Sold	Out.
" " Queen of the Isles, Scarlet and White...	40	4 00
" " finest named sorts, mixed........	15	1 00
Sweet Sultan, (Centaurea moschata atropurpurea)...	20	
Sweet William, single, mixed, fine............	15	1 00
" " double, mixed, extra...........	40	4 00
Verbena hybrida, (Defiance), scarlet..........	1 00	
" " blue.....	75	
" " Italian striped	1 00	
" " pure white, our own-growth, extra.........	1 00	
" Mammoth mixed, " " "	3 00	
" splendid, mixed...........	1 50	
" fine mixed, all colors............	75	7 50
Wall Flower, double, mixed, extra fine...:...	2 50	

ZINNIA, DOUBLE.

	PER OZ.	PER LB.
Zinnia, double, yellow......................	35	
" " deep purple...............	35	
" " violet	35	
" scarlet..................	35	
" " orange..............	35	
" " dark violet	35	
" " purple...............	35	
" " white, (alba plenissima)	35	
" " Pompon, finest mixed........	60	
" " choicest mixed............	25	2 50
" " striped or Zebra, mixed......	60	6 00

HAND GARDEN IMPLEMENTS.

FOR PRICES OF THE "PLANET JR." SEED DRILLS AND CULTIVATORS SEE PAGE 47.

THE "PLANET JR." HILL DROPPING GARDEN DRILL.

This Drill will sow in hills with perfect accuracy as well as in rows. It will sow all kinds of garden seeds from Peas and Beans down to Celery. It opens, sows, covers, rolls down and marks the next row, all at one operation. The machine holds two quarts and is adapted for all conditions of land, working especially well in fresh ground or when planting on a ridge. We can also supply a special flow attachment for sowing *onion seeds for sets,* which will open several shallow furrows side by side, making a band of plants about four inches wide. This attachment is an extra.

THE "PLANET JR."
Combined Hill Dropping Seed and Fertilizer Drill.

For several years there has been a pressing demand, especially by market gardeners and onion growers, for a machine which would not only do all that the machine just described will do, but at the same time sow fertilizers either above or below the seed as wanted and in any quantity necessary. The machine shown in this cut does this work perfectly. It works with entire regularity whether there is much or little in the Drill, and small heaps do not interfere with its regular sowing. It holds about one peck.

THE "PLANET JR." NO. 2 SEED DRILL.

Sows all garden seeds accurately at any desired thickness or depth. Opening, dropping, covering, rolling down and marking the next row all at one passage in the most perfect and reliable manner. It holds 2½ quarts. It is remarkable for simplicity and strength and for ease and perfection of work in the field. No one having use for a Seed Drill can afford to buy any other. It is the best. Truckers, market gardeners, onion growers and all who raise vegetables in quantity, should supply themselves also with the "Planet Jr." Double Wheel Hoe. (Described on page 46.)

THE "PLANET JR."
Combined Drill, Wheel Hoe, Cultivator, Rake and Plow.

THE "FIRE-FLY" WHEEL GARDEN PLOW.

Makes the care of a vegetable garden a pleasure, and 10,000 families who could not find time to keep a garden, if attempting cultivation with the ordinary hand hoe, can raise their own vegetables successfully with the "Fire Fly."

THE "PLANET JR." DOUBLE WHEEL HOE, CULTIVATOR, RAKE AND PLOW.

This very popular tool has been greatly simplified, strengthened and improved and merits the thorough admiration of every practical gardener. Each tool is sent out with a pair of rakes, a pair of hoes, a pair of cultivator teeth, a pair of four-inch sweeps, and a pair of plows. The wheels are

adjustable in height, and the arch is 14 inches high. Leaf guards (detachable), go with each machine, to be used when plants extend into a wide row. This tool is light, very simple, made of the best material and highly finished, and nothing can exceed the perfection and variety of work it performs.

"PLANET JR." PLAIN DOUBLE WHEEL HOE.

To meet a demand from Onion Growers and others who want a hoe only, we offer the Double Wheel Hoe, just described, supplied simply with one pair of long curved point hoes. This tool has the same adjustment of hoes and wheel as the above, and any or all of the other attachments may be added to this at any time, and will be found to fit.

THE "PLANET JR." GRASS EDGER.

A cheap, handy and effective Grass Edger is a treasure, and here it is; one with which you can in an hour edge beautifully the walks and the *flower and shrub beds* of an ordinary half-acre lawn. This perfect little tool does either *straight or curved* work most accurately, edging at the desired angle, and at the speed of a mile an hour.

For heavy work the frame forms a pocket just the proper size to carry a brick, which gives the needed additional weight for effectual service.

Strawberry growers will find it also a rapid and perfect tool for cutting off surplus runners. For this work the hoe may be removed.

By removing the wheel, the hoe may be used alone with great satisfaction in the vegetable garden, first cutting away from the crop, and then returning the earth.

THE "PLANET JR." SINGLE WHEEL HOE, CULTIVATOR, RAKE AND PLOW.

Great strength, easy running, simple combinations, and variety of attachments are striking features of this favorite for the season of 1892. The full equipment is shown in the cut. All the blades are steel, hardened in oil, tempered and polished. The wheel has an extra broad face, and

is readily raised and lowered, and can be attached at one side of the frame so that one can cultivate both sides of a row of small plants at one passage. For the home vegetable garden its work is exactly what is needed for the easy cultivation of crops without the aid of a horse. Its lightness strength and simplicity recommend it to all who examine it.

The "Fire=Fly" Single Wheel Hoe, Cultivator and Plow.

This popular implement has also been completely remodeled, and is greatly increased in strength and simplicity. The adjustment for depth is perfect, and for the first time, it has been arranged to hoe both sides of a row at one passage, by attaching the wheel to one side of the main frame. It is similar in all respects to the "Planet Jr." Single Wheel Hoe just described, and does the same variety of work, *excepting it is not supplied with the new Rakes and Leaf Guard.*

☞ PRICES OF "PLANET JR." GOODS, PACKED OR BOXED READY FOR SHIPMENT, AND DELIVERED AT EXPRESS OFFICE OR DEPOT IN DETROIT, MICH.

	TEL. CIPHER.	
"Planet Jr." Hill Dropping Garden Drill............................	Woodruff.....	$ 8 00
" Combined Hill Dropping Seed and Fertilizer Drill...	Weld..........	12 00
" No. 2 Drill.....................................	Windham ...	6 25
" Combined Drill, Wheel Hoe, Cultivator, etc..........	Winn	8 00
" Double Wheel Hoe, Cultivator, etc..............	Winston	5 50
" Plain Double Wheel Hoe......................	Wise...... ..	3 25
" Single Wheel Hoe.............................	Wirt	4 25
" Grass Edger.......................	Wallowa......	2 75
"Fire-Fly" Single Wheel Hoe, Cultivator and Plow.............	Woodson ...	3 85
"Fire-Fly" Wheel Garden Plow	Worth	2 00

MATTHEWS' GARDEN SEED DRILLS AND CULTIVATORS.

MATTHEWS' GARDEN SEED DRILL.

We know of no hand Garden Drill, for sowing vegetable seeds, etc., which has met with more popularity than the Matthews' Garden Seed Drill among market gardeners everywhere.

It is designed for use in field and garden. When in operation it opens the furrow, drops the seed accurately at the desired depth, covers it and lightly rolls the earth down over it, and at the same time, marks the next row.

A valuable feature in this Drill is its patent INDICATOR, with names of different seeds on it, for adjusting the Drill to sow different kinds of seed, which is done by simply turning the Indicator until the name of the seed you want to sow comes to the top. No other drill is furnished with this ingenious device. This Drill is made of the best material throughout, and is complete in all its arrangements. Price, boxed and delivered at Depot or Express Office in Detroit, Mich., $6.75. (Tel. Cipher, Yates.)

MATTHEWS' IMPROVED DRILL, CULTIVATOR AND HOE COMBINED.

Matthews' Drill, Cultivator and Hoe, Combined, is the most complete combined implement of the kind made. When used as a drill, it possesses all the features of the separate Matthews' Drill, except it is of a smaller size. It will sow all the different varieties of vegetable seeds as well as that, and when used as a cultivator or a hoe, it is substantially like the Matthews' Hand Cultivator or the Matthews' Wheel Hoe, and is fully equal to either of them. Therefore in this there is combined all three of those implements in one and it cannot fail to give the best satisfaction to any one wanting a combined implement. Price, boxed and delivered at Depot or Express Office in Detroit, Mich., $8.25. (Tel. Cipher, Yazoo.)

"Gem of the Garden" Hand Wheel Hoe and Cultivator.

This implement is offered to gardeners and others with the assurance that it is the most effective and convenient tool of the kind yet invented. Its working parts are: two Scuffle or Cutting Blades, one 4½ and one 9 inches wide; two Plows, right and left hand; five Stirring Teeth, all made of best steel. The wheel and handles of the "GEM" are both adjustable in height, while the frame is so slotted that the hoes, teeth and plows can be set in almost any position or angle. The hoes, of thin steel, and presenting nearly a straight line to the work, avoid the "dodging", so common to tools of this kind. Price, boxed and delivered at Depot or Express Office in Detroit, Mich., $3.75. (Tel. Cipher, York.)

THE WEED SLAYER.

In offering this tool we are confident from our experience with it that it is a very superior tool for use in the garden among onions, turnips, corn, potatoes, strawberries, etc., and for weeding among flowers and in gravel walks. It is light, weighing but 7 lbs.; strong, made of the best steel and iron; adjustable to any height of person, and cutting from one-half inch to one and one-half inches under ground and 7 inches wide. Price, packed and delivered at Depot or Express Office in Detroit, Mich., $1.50 each. (Tel. Cipher, Young.)

SEED BAGS.

No doubt most Seedsmen have experienced considerable difficulty (as we have) in obtaining ready-made bags suitable for Seed purposes. Most in the market are *machine made,* with more or less *imperfections,* and frequently made from *very weak and poor paper.*

The following are all designed especially for *Seed purposes* and except Nos. 11, 13 and 16, are *hand made.* The larger sizes, from 1 pint upward, are made from the *best Manilla Paper* with a high finish and are graded in weight or thickness according to size of bag. The smaller sizes are made from the finest finished paper obtainable.

Samples of all sizes furnished on application.

No.							Per 1,000
1	Miniature Pockets, White		⅞	x	2¼	inches	$ 70
3	Cream Linen		2⅛	x	3¼	"	1 00
6	"	"	2¾	x	4	"	1 25
9	"	"	3½	x	4	"	1 75
12	"	"	4	x	4¾	"	2 75
11	Manilla, Gummed	½ oz	2⅛	x	3½	"	1 00
13	"	" 1 oz	2½	x	4¼	"	1 25
16	"	" 2 oz	3	x	5½	"	1 50
15	Colored Manilla	1 oz	3¾	x	4⅝	"	2 00
18	"	" 2 oz	4½	x	5½	"	2 50
21	"	" (Square) 4 oz	4⅛	x	4⅝	"	2 00
24	"	" (Flat) 4 oz	5	x	6¼	"	3 00
27	"	" ½ pint	4½	x	5¼	"	2 25
30	"	" ½ pound	5	x	6	"	2 75
33	Unbleached Manilla	1 pint	5	x	7¾	"	2 25
36	"	" 1 pound	5½	x	8	"	2 50
39	"	" 1 quart	6½	x	9¼	"	3 25
42	"	" 3 pints	7½	x	10¼	"	4 00
45	"	" 2 quarts	8½	x	11½	"	5 25
48	"	" 3 quarts	9½	x	12½	"	6 50
51	"	" 4 quarts	10½	x	14½	"	9 00
54	"	" 6 quarts	11¾	x	16¼	"	12 00
57	"	" 8 quarts	13	x	18	"	16 00

Printing, from $1.00 to $2.50 per 1,000 extra.

D. M. FERRY & CO.,
DETROIT, MICH.

NOTICE.

By making use of the following Telegraphic words for weights and measures, together with the Telegraphic Cipher attached to each article in this list, our customers will be able to order by wire at trifling expense. The Telegraphic words for QUANTI-TIES must always PRECEDE the cipher words for Seeds, but if the same quantity of several articles is needed, the word for that quantity should be placed before the word for the first article only. For example —

"**Freight Righter Kearney, Kossuth, Lehigh.**" Means "Send by first freight Five Bushels each of Ferry's First and Best Selected, McLean's Little Gem and Champion of England Peas."

"**Express Recanter Broome, Burke, Carlton.**" Means "Ship by first express Two Pounds each of Early Jersey Wakefield (true American), Early Winnigstadt and D. M. Ferry & Co's Premium Flat Dutch Cabbage.

TELEGRAPHIC WORDS FOR WEIGHTS.

AM'T	OUNCES.	AM'T	POUNDS.	AM'T	POUNDS.	AM'T	POUNDS.
⅛	Radner.....	¼	Raffler.....	13	Rejoinder..	40	Requiter...
¼	Rapper.....	½	Raker	14	Renewer...	45	Reminder..
½	Raptor.....	¾	Rancor	15	Repealer ..	50	Reviser....
¾	Rasher.....	1	Rebutter...	16	Replier.....	55	Reader.....
1	Racer......	2	Recanter...	17	Reporter...	60	Rescinder..
2	Racker ...	3	Receiver...	18	Reprover..	65	Renter....
3	Radiator...	4	Reckoner..	19	Respirator	70	Reliever....
	....	5	Recliner ...	20	Retainer..	75	Revolver...
	....	6	Recorder..	21	Retriever..	80	Ritter .....
	....	7	Rector.....	22	Revealer...	85	Ribalder...
	....	8	Refiner....	23	Revenger..	90	Riser......
	....	9	Reflector..	24	Reviewer...	95	Rigeur.....
	....	10	Reformer..	25	Reviler.....	100	Rewarder..
	....	11	Registrar..	30	Repulsor...	150	Repiner...
	....	12	Regular....	35	Retour.....	200	Rescuer....

TELEGRAPHIC WORDS FOR MEASURES.

AM'T	BUSHELS.	AM'T	BUSHELS.	AM'T	BUSHELS.	AM'T	BUSHELS.
¼	Rebuker....	10	Rioter......	21	Ruiner.....	60	Resorter...
½	Reasoner..	11	Ripper.....	22	Ruler......	65	Rowler.. ..
¾	Rearer......	12	Robber.....	23	Rumbler...	70	Rounder...
1	Rhymer.....	13	Rocker....	24	Ruminator.	75	Runner....
2	Rider......	14	Roister.....	25	Rummager	80	Roader....
3	Rifler......	15	Roller.. ...	30	Resignor..	85	Rouncer...
4	Rigger.....	16	Rooster....	35	Roadster...	90	Rugger ....
5	Righter....	17	Rover.......	40	Resolver...	95	Rouser....
6	Rigor.......	18	Rower.....	45	Rouper.....	100	Rusher....
7	Rimer......	19	Rubber.....	50	Rumor.....	150	Replacer..
8	Ringer....	20	Rudder.....	55	Roguer....	200	Restorer...
9	Rinser.....						

Early Red Valentine, Imp. Round Pod.

We challenge comparison of our stock of this very valuable Bean with that of any in the country.